The Commonality in Success?

Perspective of a 21 year old.

Disclaimer

The contents of this book are based solely on a positive and unique thought invoking/introspecting ideology.

The book written is to throw light on what the common point in success is rather than trying to ignite any harsh comments or misunderstandings. So take it the meant way

The book's understanding is solely based on the reader's interpretation. Do not take the point of the book to somewhere or some idea that it does not represent.

PS: ignore the grammatical mistakes and just focus on the concept, not the detail of writing. Thanks.

FOREWORD

Before jumping in to the contents of this book, one thing to ask is, "why do you guys think that there is a question mark in the title"?

It is there because, in overall, there could be n number of common points in success, ranging from passion, hard work, discipline, persistence or perseverance, talent etc. But each success story while it might not have a few of those things, one thing that it for sure has is what you are about to read.

So the main reason why there is a question mark is, for the reader to think what is the common point?, then read this book and to see whether he/she agrees with what's written and gain a new sight of perspective.

CONTENTS

Let's jump directly to the point – Rebelliousness

How Rebelliousness, Let's see

- The way of thinking

- The fight

- The its & bits

- Satisfaction & Feel

How build rebelliousness

- Perspective change & evolve

- Debate

- Don't agree & accept immediately

- Ready to accept and agree

- Do

Thoughts to ponder upon

Conclusion

Motivational Stuff

Acknowledgements

About the author

REBELLIOUSNESS

Yes, that is the commonality/common point in all success stories, Rebelliousness. And before we move on, what do you think is the meaning of that word? The meaning, not the definition, is asked because if you are to go based on the definition, it may not make much sense. Sometimes you have to give your own meaning to things to get a better grasp. You have to create your own mould and then base your ideas on it.

The definition provided in the Cambridge dictionary is as follows:

"The act of opposing the ideas of the people in authority and planning to change the system"

"The quality of being difficult to control and not behaving in the way that other people expect"

The definition is very much relatable to what the message being shared is, yet it still lacks something. It lacks the personal touch of each and every individual and their personal meanings & inputs. Rebelliousness is just not a word which can be defined in a particular sense or it isn't loosely the ability to oppose or not being able to control or challenge authority. It is much more than just a word. It is a sense of thought for some, someone's whole life ideology or one's adrenaline rush or a million other things. It is something that no one can articulate into clear cut words.

The only way that it can be explained is as simple. You know how liquids are, taking water for example, it does not have its own shape, but rather, it takes the shape of the container or vessel it is kept or poured into. The same way is this, rebelliousness gets its meaning from a particular person's thought/ideology and working process and no other way do I think makes more sense.

The idea is that you do something against the common flow or general path to achieve something that cannot be done just by following a simple path or set of rules and guidelines. One needs to go against those very rules, thought patterns, common pathways to achieve something not all have. It is about making the change many people only talk about or doing something that others feel cannot be done, or accomplishing something that you yourself think is extremely hard, or setting your mind on a particular thing and making sure you go up against anything or everything that will lead your mind to go in another direction.

More interesting is the fact that each and every one of us has had rebelliousness inside us, but it is just that many or most of us then tend to lose it or that tendency gets reduced as time flows. Let me give you a few examples to prove how every single one of us has it.

The first and foremost example is the fact that you were born. It takes only one sperm for pregnancy i.e. every time someone is born, that particular sperm specimen has defeated (harsh word) /rebelled against millions of other sperm cells to reach the egg. There, even before you were born, you had it in you.

Let's take another example. Take a baby who is learning to walk. Now he/she does fall quite a few times, but its nature is such that it rebels with its own mind to get up again. If not, the kid would never have learned to walk. The same goes for almost anything with babies; they are conditioned with that attitude, like say when they need something they rebel by crying or crawling around or annoying their elders.

It is only after we gain a conscience that we lose that ability to rebel and we start to go with the flow. That is where, if you try to go out of the way and do or learn something, whether you succeed in that task is not guaranteed, but the experience you gain is invaluable and that is guaranteed.

The whole idea of being an outcast in thought or action is actually an evolving one and prehistoric. Take any historical game/time-changing event. It starts with the idea of being different or with the idea that the already existing norm is wrong and needs to be changed. Take revolutions, for example, be it French or Russian etc, or take the wars and freedom fighters of each nation from Rani Lakshmi Bai to Martin Luther King Junior. The common point is the same in all of these examples and even gods, for that sake, even gods are in a way rebels, because what they envision for the people, the greater good, required thinking which was/is different and rebellious of nature or something not following the normal norm.

It is the spirit to do something different for some cause, which is positively life-altering either for yourself or for the ones surrounding you or even both.

I saw an Instagram post (do not remember the account, sorry) saying "I believe, by nature, that all humans are philosophers. We're all innately curious creatures bewildered by existence, full of questions and farfetched ideas. But early on in life, those who came before us indoctrinate us into their mould, and we sink further into hand-me-down beliefs, we lose sight of the most important thing, our wonder. We see ourselves as mundane, almost repulsive and our philosophic disposition gives way to systematic behavior and standard norms & procedures set by the society. Life becomes trivial: we don't ask questions. Instead, we salute politicians, scientists, experts, religions, god and march towards death without pausing to reflect."

The above-mentioned lines truly summarize everything said until now about the rebellious attitude of humans in a very subtle and nonchalant way. I couldn't have found a better way to explain it than these lines. Completely resonate and connect with those lines.

The whole idea here is to tell people to think differently, to improve the quality of your life, for the people around you and humanity as a whole. Just because some book says that being rebellious or thinking that way is the first and foremost step to success, don't go ahead and start fights with everything or everyone or do something which degrades or destroys your life. All things mentioned here are to bring a sense of understanding where you think outside of the box for creativity, studies, business or improving your quality of life or to get a sense of satisfaction and stability at all levels, be it physical, emotional, psychological, and/or spiritual. The narrative here is that when you go against your own thinking and the world's to create something or change something, that's a sign that whether you pass or fail, it does not matter, you are now part of the commonality of success.

How – Let's See

Step 1 – The way of thinking

A machine works based on how it is built and what parts perform what functions, or a software works based on how it is programmed. The same way is the idea of rebelling, wherein our mind has always been made to evolve and change into something which we aren't or something better than what we were the previous day. When we do not use it (machine/software/anything) for a long time, it gets rusty or outdated or sometimes damaged and, likewise we mustn't get rusty by getting accustomed to a common path. We need to work with our system to do stuff that requires change and that causes change and for that, we have to start thinking differently and out of our comfort zone. Many greats of our time have it in them and constantly work hard to be the better and different version of them just by starting to think about it and how to achieve it. Throughout we will look at examples which show us and prove that the common point in all success stories starts with the idea of being rebellious and thinking uniquely. Start to think differently even for simple things, because once you start that, then you automatically get into the groove and that becomes the basis for when a particular idea ("the one") which you think is a game changer transpires.

No success comes just from the saying "they did it and succeeded, so let's follow that and we will too". What you see is the end result but not the process of it. The process is the most important aspect and the journey is the most enjoyable and knowledgeable period where you will gain the invaluable experiences you need. The end goal is just a mere product of multiple things brought together.

Also, the most important and vital piece of information that one needs to know is that when you read the title and see the word success, it does not just mean becoming a millionaire or billionaire or getting rich but towards any goal. Success is basically you winning something, be it work, sports, job, life, a game, your career, or any other thing.

"Not all treasure is silver and gold mate" (a movie dialogue from "Pirates of the Caribbean: The curse of the Black Pearl produced by Jerry Bruckheimer) perfectly encompasses the lines of the previous paragraph. Each and every one has a different end result which will have different processes and journeys. So, while you envision the end result, the goal or the premise here is to start from scratch (which most of us have to) and that scratch or starting point is, the way of thinking.

Once I saw an Instagram reel, in which a guy says, that on a particular given day maybe, your best is at par with the best of a GOAT (Greatest of All Time) and that it is very much plausible that you could beat them at their play at a particular given day, but what's more important is that the reason they are the GOAT and it is difficult to reach where they are is because their week beats your week, their year beats your year, their decade beats your decade, their two decades beats your decade and so it is their work ethic, the effort they put in for a long period of time that is unparallel and continuous which provides them the advantage and the thing is that their thought process is so damn strong that they go against their own heart to be better than they were. Do you really think that these greats want to or wanted to work out each and every day for all days or that they practice in such a way? No, but they rebel against their own minds and put in the effort that is needed for them to make sure that later they don't have to or some random person does not beat them or outwork them.

The way of thinking should be such that, after some point, your thoughts & ethics should lead and pave the way for you while punching out anything else (negative) and providing you with the sense of satisfaction that you crave and require.

While reading this you can think "Ah, easier said than done". But, that's where you are different. At the least you are trying and not just preaching stuff and to those who aren't, start. Anything that you do should have your own personal touch or mark on it and it should reflect your perspective or thought process and you as a person. Uniqueness, rebelliousness matter to me a lot because that is what differentiates me from the rest and brings in a sense of satisfaction. (I use this mantra for everything from projects to assignments to even thinking about some random thing)

The higher the challenge or process or work difficulty, more the sense of satisfaction when you achieve the end result. It does not matter (obviously you feel sad) whether the end result is in my favor, but the process in itself provides that utility.

Note - I find that it is easier to connect with some topic or somebody when you use a lot of examples to explain something and I tend to use a lot of examples and that is what we will do here too, so that I can try maximum to connect with the reader and explain better what I want to convey.

For me, that's still a success. For those who think that success has a clear definition, you are wrong my friend. It is you who defines what success means to you. The way of thinking is the first and foremost factor which will help build the idea that success is just an achievement of the goal you defined and the journey is the pathway/road you choose to reach your destination and the way of thinking is the mode of transport for the ride.

A more relatable example would be the fact that I am writing this book. As an individual, I am neither a book person nor do I prefer reading books, but that's why this is a challenge. Writing this book is me cultivating the way of thinking (thinking differently) and harvesting the rebellious attitude we are discussing. I am not sure how things are going to pan out but I enjoyed the process and have put in my best.

Everyone should feel that they have that uniqueness among them. To throw another perspective is, considering the whole set of humans as the common point i.e. all are human beings but the thing that differentiates us is basically us, our looks (which also sometimes astonishingly can match another random human being), our thoughts, our ideologies make us the different one in the whole common set, that itself is what the book is about. You have succeeded automatically without any effort put in. So if, among 8 BILLION people in the world, you are the only one like you, why not have thoughts about an assignment or business or anything like that, by adding in your uniqueness to it. If it pans out, it does. If not, it doesn't, but you did something rebellious that's out of your normal way. That's the experience which will always help you achieve success, keep you humble and grounded.

Start the way of thinking differently and see how it works out for you. Hells YEAH!

Step 2 – The Fight

Have you ever wondered about seeing some famous personality on social media, like how he/she is living his/her life to the fullest and enjoying himself/herself and looks like he/she has nothing to worry about?

Well, to answer that, let me try to paint another picture and see if i can bring around a change in thought and induce what the second step talks about in you.

Let's take an exam scenario. So you have an exam tomorrow and you take all the course materials and the books and what not and set it up, and just stare at them and hope that everything goes into your head (without actually reading or practicing or studying) and you ace the exam. Do you think it's possible? No, of course not and for obvious reasons, that you did not study/ did not put any effort. Just having a thought does not count. That is just step one. You need to complete the chain and get to the final point. Likewise, if you want the thing you desire, you need to fight for it, the fight that many think about but never actually engage in.

That's step 2. Just having a rebellious ideology doesn't work. The thing you need with that idea is the rebellious work ethic, the fight against everything or anything, a strong work attitude, the will to act on the rebellious idea that you had.

This has multiple points of view which we'll discuss now.

One easy example which comes to mind while I am writing this portion is Virat Kohli. Considered one of the greatest batsmen in cricket of the modern era, having record-breaking numbers, one of the most followed Indian personalities across social media channels, very influential, a commanding alpha male and has an extremely disciplined work ethic and is one of the fittest and finest fielders in Indian cricket. Now do you think he just had it? No, he created it for himself and rebelled his way to success and the position he is while not taking anything for granted. The following are his words:

> "It (the turnaround) happened in 2012. I was eating anything that came inside. I was finishing candy packets, 40 pieces, and three packets a week. I was eating and sleeping horribly, my habits were all

over the place. I finished the IPL, I remember I went home, came out of the shower, saw myself in the mirror and I was ashamed.

Literally, I saw myself and thought I was looking at another human being. Then I told myself, if you want to play cricket at the highest level, this is not the way you can manage.

Everything about my diet and training changed from the next day onwards and it became an obsession."

He also says in another interview that the first six months are the hardest (I am not sure of this) when you are turning it around and you have to go to war with every fiber of your being and stay strong and once you get through, it becomes your second nature and leaving that becomes difficult. Changing yourself and a battle against the mind & heart are the hardest challenges anyone's ever going to face because you are in competition with your own mind. A battle against others is not that challenging because in the end you can just say or have the mindset that I am the best and leave or needn't prove anyone. So you just leave it, but you can't cheat your mind or the heart and it is extremely difficult to go up against your natural flow.

If you don't put in the grind and are just an individual with all thoughts and resolutions but no action, then those are lost opportunities and it embodies the sentence "could have would have should have". You need to act; nobody else is going to do it for you. To reach the top, the pinnacle, you need to rebel the eff off.

Think of the movie "The Pursuit of Happyness adapted from the book of the same name by Chris Gardener", a movie starring Will Smith (based on the real life story of Chris Gardner, a self-made salesman-turned-stock broker-turned-philanthropist) who went through untold hard times before finally scraping his way to success. The whole movie very clearly defines about the rebellious nature and resilient fight attitude and using that to overturn your life. He went through the darkest times and he still knew that he could get out of it, while the whole world, even his wife, didn't think so and with his boy by his side. The attitude to not throw towel in, not to give in, while the world thinks you should and thinks you are done, is what shows that if you fight on with the right mindset, things will start to turn.

But the scene which we will focus on is the scene where his boy narrates a story about how a man's drowning and three boats pass by but he doesn't climb on and eventually dies. Then when he meets god and asks about not helping him, while getting back the answer from god that, what you see is the help you get (That the three boats where basically the help he sent). Don't just sit and think god will come directly.

It is you who has got to do something with the visible/available resources; you get a boat, climb, do the work, put in the effort, nobody else is going to do it for you, not god for sure. It's just a belief that god helps; while in reality it's you. You can't expect the food to taste perfect with you just standing there without adding salt and thinking that the salt will be added there magically. No, you have got to add it, put the work in, think only about the process and outwork yourself and convert your pulling down mindset to a rebellious one.

A message from the Late Stan Lee (Co-creator of Spiderman)

"If you have an idea that you genuinely think is good, don't let some idiot talk you out of it." Sound advice from Stan Lee who adds that "Whatever you do, give it your best shot and you'll be glad you did."

The idiot could be anyone in the world. Work it out; it was you who got the idea. That means you did give it some thought and now fight for it, pour your heart out.

So Step On and bring it on!!

Step 3 – The its and bits

It's the little things that make big things happen or changes one's whole life around. While we have spoken about the commonality factor and that you have to fight and work for the process, the things that we do often on a regular basis/daily basis are the ones that don't get recognized. Those are the its and bits you need to work on your way to victory. Also, in this section we discuss about the people who are already this way. So let's take a separate viewpoint and see things from the already rebellious side.

There are lots of little things that happen to have the biggest implications. Let's look at a few examples, starting from my personal experience.

In my 12th grade, in two of my exams for two different subjects, the silliest of mistakes caused me to lose marks. I did not read a question in one and misread the question in the other. It's a small thing to read the question paper, but if only I had paid more attention to it. Didn't think of checking the paper too, which all students should, and after that, I always did check.

(To all the students out there, if you ever read this, check how many questions are there and read the question slowly before answering it. It helps.)

These are small things which look like they don't matter or have the serious of impacts. But they do. Things like discipline, being thorough, up-skilling or upgrading/updating you to the required skills which will help achieve the goal, communication skills, small changes in habits, challenges/bets and games related to it, taking a break, speaking about it to somebody, all of these are the small its and bits you got to do so that you reach your final destination.

Did you know that Bill Gates, co-founder of Microsoft, takes two weeks' time off every year from everything (tech & communication less/nil) to some quiet place to recover from his hectic schedule, boost morale and productivity. It is a think week per say.

Jeff Bezoz, the founder of Amazon, schedules all his important meetings before 10 AM because he is most active & attentive during that period and by later that evening he is worn out and doesn't want to take any important decisions in a worn out condition.

These are small things which these people do because they understand its importance and its value in their life.

The Late Kobe Bryant used to say that he starts his workout at 4 AM and then takes a break, works out again later and then a break, he is back at it again and the same. He says, just by starting at 4, he is at an advantage and his ideology is that if you are to do this, after a few years, you gain so much head start than anybody that no one can easily match you at your game.

All this sounds simple and some you of may even think that it contradicts the theme of the book, but that's how it is. Sometimes it is wise to accept that you do not always need the rebellious spirit. We will brush up on this in a later section. It is the way you do and think about stuff that is rebellious, which is how every successful story is. That starting point is the common factor, and none of it is common among any individual. Sometimes you need to contradict the already contradicted. Think about it.

Sometimes all you need to cultivate that spirit is a small & simple thing, an hour alone with your thoughts, that's it, just that. Everyday sit for whatever time you have or get. It is not necessary that it has got to be an hour, there isn't a time limit, it could be any amount of time, and start to think about a random topic and contradict it and prove yourself wrong or the topic wrong and in that debate anything goes. A simple thing to sound, but that brings in a new approach and a difference in your thought process.

The idea of this book just about came as a challenge to me, the challenger being myself. So here's the story, I couldn't sleep and I tried everything but to no avail, so just staring at the fan, out of nowhere it struck me, why not write a book about something like this and finish it with the least amount of time and publish it. And here it is. So, you see, sometimes all big things (for me it is) may come from the most random scenarios, simple thoughts, some game you play with your friends or some food or just about anything.

Let's look at another example.

Take the game of chess into consideration. Which piece is the most important?

Of course it is the King. Which piece is considered not so powerful? It's the pawn. They may not be spoken about a lot, but it is one of the most interesting pieces on the board.

Which piece can change to another after reaching a certain place on the board? It's the pawn again. While otherwise it is not the strongest, it moves only one step at a time, but once it reaches the end, it becomes one of your greatest allies.

But to reach the end of the board, it takes only one step at a time and the whole process is time-consuming and repetitive, but that doesn't mean it is not necessary, so doing things over and over again is vital. Don't be afraid or disappointed of doing the same thing again and again. Sometimes things take time.

Burj Khalifa, the tallest building in the world, wasn't built in a day.

Likewise, these its and bits are like pawns. When individually looked at, it does not mean much or doesn't seem like it is important, but once you start to recognize it and give it importance, it will be your greatest ally in helping you achieve your goal. (Saving your king while beating the opponent's king)

So, while you should fight to save your king (the end goal), you should also focus on the small things because they are the basics and consistency in those things will help you grow and meet the end. These its and bits (pawns of chess) could be anything from practicing your game every day or meeting with employees regularly or up-skilling yourself consistently. While we are focusing on and discussing the its and bits, the other pieces are equally important too and only when all the pieces work together using one strategy can you achieve success. So don't ignore anything, neither the small its and bits nor the big moves of the end goal.

If you have ever eaten a full-course South Indian meal, you will know that while the rice and the sambar or any other kuzhambu (pronounced as kollambuu, or spicy gravy in English) is the main dish, the side dishes are the ingredients that enhance or make the meal a meal. The side dishes are the appalams, the poriyals, the sweet, the pickle or even that dried chilli (I don't like it). Just the rice and sambar becomes rather plain but if added with these side dishes, it gets the flavor, the variety, the richness in taste. It is the same way with the thought and work, the small its and bits get you to where you need to go and give the final goal an enrichment.

And if you haven't eaten a proper South Indian meal, you are missing out, so TRY IT!!!

Step 4 – Satisfaction & Feel

Any work we do in our life is all about making sure that we are satisfied with it, we feel happy & content doing it, knowing that we are doing the work we love. Every major success story and the person behind it would have the same thing to recommend: find your passion. Find something that you are ready to go the distance to accomplish. The feeling and the satisfaction you get doing that work is generally achieved by those who are rebellious, and do not follow the ordinary path. You should look forward to doing something. The word "passion" basically means a strong feeling, a strong feeling towards anything. We are going to get to know more about that.

Sometimes what you are passionate about does not fall under the common corridor, so you already have the rebellious spirit and you have or are ready to put up a fight and you see your execution. Then, what about after that?

Here we'll discuss handling feelings after the job, i.e. post fight or post execution feelings. Things could pan out the way you like, creating a positive feeling while, if not, a negative feeling.

Satisfaction here is based on each individual's own ideology & perspective on what they define their success as. Some are just satisfied by the process and some by the result and how you have defined your end result again changes how you feel. Even failures sometimes provide a feeling of content. So that's why you hear all successful people say "be more focused on the process, not the end result. Take care of the process and do justice to it." Once you start focusing on the process, you have changed your definition of success; you are now not bothered by what the outcome will be. Yes, you will work for it to be in your favor, but if it isn't, then you will be able to handle things better.

As humans, we tend to look more at where we will reach or have reached rather than how. You need to rebel against the general human tendency to both success and failures, to not get over excited during successes and overly sad during failures. You need to face failures to cultivate that spirit. It is never going to be the same always; it's a failure now, not necessary that it has to be the same next time. So think and act and try to understand the situation, and then emote. That is why you would have heard almost all the really successful people say, be ready to fail or embrace failure, or failure/mistakes are the most important.

You know how people say failure is important and you learn a lot from it and it is very important for failures to happen and to face rejection, the idea or premise behind it is very simple.

Take a child, for example, and let us say he/she is playing with something that may cause him/her some harm. We advise them not to play with that particular thing, but they don't listen, but once if they are hurt, they would never do that again, because they have had that experience with them. What doesn't kill you makes you stronger. (I can argue about that statement in general, but in this POV it makes sense. We will discuss that in later sections.) The same way when you do something and fail, you now know what not to do. That is the reason you hear that a lot and also why it works. If you want another reference, you can watch the movie Captain America: The First Avenger, produced by Marvel Studios based on the comics of the same name, the scene where the doctor tells why he chose Steve (who understands not having power and what its importance is) over everybody else.

Tom hanks, an actor, once said, I think I saw this on an Instagram reel (again I do not remember the account, sorry), saying the thing he wished he knew earlier was "this too shall pass", saying, you feel great, feel like you know all the answers or you feel sad, feel like nothing's going your way, in both scenarios "this too shall pass". Nothing will stay how it is. Nothing's constant except change. See now, that's again the mind fighting against what the general formula of feelings is. To be neutral in feelings and knowing that if you have succeeded, be happy at that moment, but work harder, because there will always be the rebellious ones who are ready to outsmart or outwork you and knowing that you have failed, be sad, yes, but then work again, because there is something that we have not done right that particular time and that is why you aren't at the place you want you to be. [There will be a few who say, more than that you need to be at the right place at the right time and luck and all that is right and makes sense but that is a separate topic that we aren't going into in this theme, but feel free to introspect on that thought]

In general, feelings control us and based on them we react, but if you actually start to fight that and make sure that you are in control, then my friend, you have reached a separate new level & understanding, because now you control how you react, not your emotions, and that's a sign of a strong human being, with the rebellious spirit at heart and if you put in the work not thinking about the result but just work for the satisfaction that your mind and heart requires, you will become a force to be reckoned with.

So again, always work for the satisfaction. Do things that make you content, make you feel like you are on top of the world. But it definitely is a fact, that the feeling and the satisfaction that you will get when you prove yourself wrong or others wrong and get the job done, nothing can match that. It is like playing badminton and you have won a 50 rally point. The work you put in and then the winning point. Once you start on this path, this is the biggest addiction and you start cultivating the mindset to go big and once you do it never fades away but becomes a habit.

Have simple ideologies which match your feelings to help you provide the utility you desire to make you stay on the path or change the path when necessary, like if people are saying it can't be done or argue with you, it is only because there isn't any formula yet or it hasn't been achieved yet, so you create one and show how it's done.

Contradictory to whatever we have discussed right until now is also a fact that sometimes when you go out of the way, it is not necessary, and when somebody in your circle says not to pursue it, you need to listen and maybe accept that. Rebelliousness isn't just always fighting and arguing, but it is to know that you can and will wherever necessary and where you won't.

Sometimes you rebel against others.

Sometimes you rebel against yourself to not rebel.

The Boston Consulting Group (BCG) matrix is the perfect example where I connect the four segments into my way of understanding rebelliousness and to encompass all of the written ideas above.

The BCG matrix is put simply, a framework that helps companies decide how to prioritize their different businesses. Its four quadrants, each with its own unique symbol, represent a certain degree of profitability: question marks, stars, dog and cash cows. By assigning each business to one of these four categories, executives could then decide where to focus

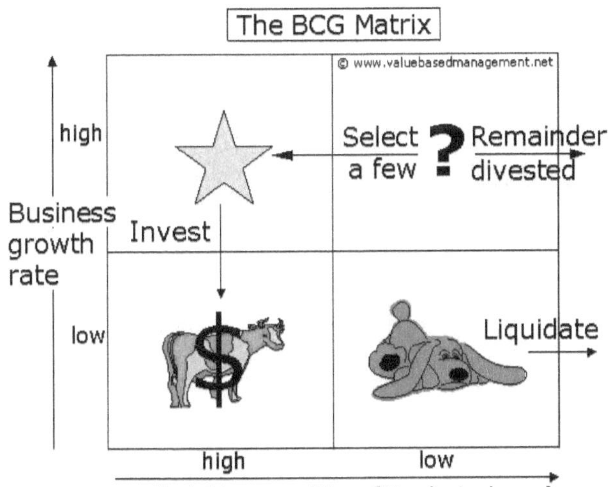

their resources and capital to generate the most value, as well as where to cut their losses.

So you start with the question mark (problem child) or, as I put it, rebelliousness generation point.

Then there are the star and cash cow positions, here you put up a fight believing in yourself and the idea and against the world and that the idea could be milked to give out the best results.

The last is the dog. You should also know when to let go if need be, for both personal and professional benefit, likewise for the benefit of the mind & heart and its peace. There may be n number of reasons why, so knowing when to back off is also the rebellious sport one needs to be successful.

Also, the last thing that I wanted to put in this section is a theory I have devised called **"The Moving Train Anomaly"**, which explains feelings in context with social media culture. A lot of the time for a lot of people, seeing others on social media induces a demoralizing feeling, making us feel like we haven't or aren't doing anything in life or moving forward but others are. So this theory is for those. Let me explain

Think you are inside a train,

You see outside. What do you see? Everything's moving right but

Does it mean it is? No, not completely.

Now are you moving? Answers', again both yes and no

While you are actually at constant, sitting at one place on the train while the train's moving, therefore in a way you are moving too. ------- same way, sometimes it may feel like you aren't doing anything and that maybe true, and if it is that way, then think of something and do, don't sit idle, let the rebellious bird out of the cage, and if you are already doing something don't get saddened just because it looks like somebody is doing better. Chances are they are or, chances are they aren't too.

Again, because the train is moving, the outside looks as if it is moving too, but in reality it isn't, but if you do see some roads, then yes, the outside, i.e. the vehicles or the people, they are moving too. ------- Don't get saddened just because it looks like the world is moving and climbing the ladder, sometimes what looks like something doesn't necessarily mean it is true but at the same time if they are moving, consider them as a inspiration, wish them well and all success, because you now know what they went through because you are in their shoes now. They were resilient enough and now you will be too.

The social media culture has brought on some weird crap thoughts and insecurities which are actually nothing but a mirage, a hoax and, also, the fact is that there is a lot of unnecessary talk around us which can hinder people's feelings, but in reality,, are just basic baseless words and to silence those words is very important which in turn induces a perspective change among many which is extremely required and that is what we are going to discuss next. Don't get demoralized by something that you actually don't know whether is true or false. Keep the feel, to you, the truths and inspirations. I hope "The Moving Train Anomaly" actually gives you a new sense of perspective about understanding, satisfaction and feelings and makes you move ahead towards success.

So think NEW, HOP & MOVE ON!!!!

Until now, we have looked at how rebelliousness is the common point in all success stories in detail and also looked at steps that take place on the way to success in regard to rebelliousness.

Now moving on, we see how to inculcate that rebelliousness attitude and spirit in our minds and what are those few itsy bitsy things here and there that we can do extra to bring upon that attitude and thinking mindset. To be different, you need to start getting your own perspectives on each and every thing and that has to be one that you create for yourself.

Michael Phelps, the most successful Olympian (swimming) in the history of the tournament, with 28 medals out of which 23 are gold and 8 won in a single edition (2008) of the tournament.

Do you know what made him achieve that and what his thought/perspective was?

We'll get to that in the next segment. How to get that attitude/mindset or how does it become our instinct or primary nature? The answer follows with the first aspect: Perspective.

How build rebelliousness

Perspective change & Evolve

Before we jump onto what the thought process of Michael Phelps was, let me just, for the clear understanding, define what perspective actually means. Based on the Oxford dictionaries

"The ability to think about problems and decisions in a reasonable way without exaggerating them"

Or

"Your opinion or attitude towards something"

So with that let's start on. Michael himself says that the whole thing started with just one dream or goal and that was to be the GOAT (Greatest of All Time). So do you think that was just enough? No, here is where the fight and perspective get combined. His attitude towards the goal was unshaken. For 5 years, he went without a single break in his workout i.e. 365 days a year, not a single break, and the fact is that he just simply did not like to do it every day. There were many days where he just did not want to get out of bed, but against all odds, he fought against his urges and did workout. What you want to do on the days you don't want to do anything shows your true potential/power and helps you move forward.

What separates the great or greatest from the good is the fact that they can be rebellious against themselves. In simple words, when the going gets tough, the tough get going. They are ready to sacrifice all the fun, pleasure, roaming, hanging out with friends, anything else which doesn't lead them to their goal for the all the things that they don't like doing yet do, for their own greater good.

The point to note is their perspective on what they consider as sacrifice. For them, leaving out all that stuff is no big deal, it is not a sacrifice for them but part of the process and the path they choose, a path not a lot choose and, for them, it is basically like breathing or eating food. It is part and parcel of their thought process, the path and for people like them, that isn't a sacrifice but more like fuel to start the engine and roar towards success with as max **RPM** as possible.

Let's take another example. When you grow, you lose your milk teeth for the permanent ones. Now you don't consider it sacrifices, it is rather just the natural flow of the body or the nature of the human teeth. The same is the scenario here. Those aren't sacrifices, rather moves for greatness and success. You need to prepare yourselves in such a way that you become a shell, where the not-so-needed thoughts don't penetrate in. Perspective is not a virtue but the way you are. Perspective is basically your basis of living. How you forge yourself depends on you and only you and your way of viewing things.

That is where we come to an interesting topic which I feel will completely change the basis of your thinking process, your thought analogy, ideology or any other logy which sounds cool here.

We are going to discuss about personality tests. These are tools, typically in the form of questionnaires, designed to assess human personality. A lot of you reading this might have taken one like Myers Briggs or 16 personality factor questionnaire or the big 5 personality test etc. The premise is that you answer some questions based on which the test provides you with a personality type. For example, whether you are introverted or judgmental or are logical etc.

It's just that, I feel no personality type can be defined. Yes, you could categorize and put it in words, but what you have to understand is that you need to figure it out by understanding yourself, not because some test said so.

I'll give you an example of it. Consider that we are friends and you know that I do not like beetroot (actually true, don't like it). Now, supposedly, a random person tells you that your friend likes beetroot. Would you agree? No, you won't agree right.

Because that isn't true and you know that because you know me and the fact that a random person said it, you for sure won't agree. That's the same feeling I have about these tests. I know that they are curated and everything, but how can a bunch of questions decide what your personality is? You may choose the answers to those questions without giving them a serious thought. Doesn't mean that's your personality type. Based on how you choose each time you get a very different personality type which sometimes you tend to believe is your type, while actually it isn't.

Your perspective on things can't be quantified or calculated. You are who you are and it can change. So, every time some change happens within yourself or the way you think, the way you answer the question changes, the method of answering differs each and every time.

Personality at its core never changes, you are the same, it is the additional thoughts that change and that's why the only way you can know your personality type is by getting to know yourself.

You can deliberately choose to answer it differently than you feel and get something totally unrelated to you. Therefore, no questionnaire in the world can describe what kind of person you are. Your close circle can but some random tests, I don't think so.

Simply put, you are who you are.

These personality tests most of the times don't even have the options you want. It could be that you feel all the options make sense or none do or you want to choose a few of the all. What are we supposed to do then?

To describe this, I have a theory which I call **"The Oil-Water Glass Scenario"**. Basically, this is my perspective on options and the whole premise of the personality test being just a manipulative questionnaire which knows nothing about you.

Take a question which has options: glass of oil and glass of water. You can choose only one glass.

For me, I would choose a glass which contains both water and oil and the fact that they are in the same glass, so it makes it one glass. Yes, both the liquids don't mix but they are in one glass. Sometimes we require both the things that don't mingle (symbolism for "contradictory options") but it is in one glass.

Now that's the problem with a lot of questions and that's where I start scratching my head, because both the options feel right and there is no option where either you could choose both or create one or select none of those. But many people think that they have to select one and based on that answer, the test reveals a personality type which you know isn't based on actual thought or actual input.

People need to change their perspective on these personality tests because, overall, these personality types hinder the ability to think uniquely and groups' people into similar categories, while each and every individual is different, their thought process is different and to achieve success they have to start thinking high and different and choose roads which are difficult and not common.

You need to start evolving and trying to be better than yesterday, have new ideologies, test out old ones and mend a few ones and create some new ones. What you were yesterday is not what you are today and certainly won't be tomorrow. When you know change is the only constant, why not try to be good and better than before. Evolving is understanding that everyone has their own thoughts and perspectives which they feel are right and in certain areas that could be right for you too.

I really do hope that "The Oil-Water Glass Scenario" helps people who just answer questions for the sake of answering and choose options which they don't believe in, understand that, the answer which then arrives from those tests is not the true you. Don't accept it and kill your uniqueness and get into a misunderstanding about what your personality is or who you are.

As an individual, one needs to start thinking about each and everything from your true ideology and not just a random path which is followed by many. Only you are in your shoes and only you see what you see, nobody else does. So no random person can say what kind you are.

One person's cup of tea is another person's poison, right, but why can't it also be that one person's poison is another person's tea? Why shouldn't it be that way? There could be a scenario where the person is immune to that poison or something. It's your take on things vs. other people's take on things. (All of this is considering the proverb at its face value)

Personally me, I like to argue about something that is the generally followed norm or that society follows without actually giving it some serious thought and consideration. If it's possible that those norms and the generally followed principles can be questioned and broken, then I would definitely like to try and do it. In turn, the satisfaction from doing so is unmatchable. Why is it necessary to follow some made-up rule or proverb by some guy 1000 years ago? If somebody challenges me with something that they think can't be done, I'll try whatever is possible to do it and I take that challenge. I do that for myself because I love doing it and it's not like I know I am going to succeed. I may fail (high chances), but that's not going to stop me from trying. Trying is itself the first success for me.

There are many pictures where some see one thing while others see another thing. For example, the rabbit duck image [You can find

n number of these on Google]. Now, just because you see one thing doesn't necessarily mean others have to see it that way.

They could see a different thing. Sometimes you can see either all the things & not just one or how many ever there are in that particular image, or at times, you can even see something that others think isn't there or the creator of that image wouldn't have intended to add in the first place. Just because you see one thing doesn't make it the right thing. You're right, but it doesn't mean that the other person is wrong.

The same way, when you do think of something that is against all others, you need to stick to it and keep your mind and perspective wide open while giving it your all and how you develop this kind of perspective (the odd/different thinking, rebellious and unique mindset one) on thoughts/ideas/things is by speaking.

If you change the way you look at things, the things you look at change.

Debate

Before we jump in, let us actually understand what debate means and its value in this context. There are a lot of meanings for the word debate. The Oxford dictionary states the meaning of "debate" as

"A formal discussion of an issue at a public meeting or in a parliament. In a debate, two or more speakers express opposite views and then there is often a vote on the issue."

But it also has other meanings too. Debate also means an argument or a discussion expressing different opinions. So when we talk about debate, we are going to focus on the second meaning and not the first one. Not the one with rules and then timings and timeouts and other various procedures then finally voting and winner decisions. No. No. No

Here debate means just arguing, for and against a topic, that's it. Be hell bent on proving yourself right and the other person wrong **only** during the argument period. Also, be open to knowing that you could be wrong too or that you know very little and there is still a lot to learn. A person is wise enough when knows that he/she actually knows nothing (is a fool).

But this debate does come with some conditions. And why debate? Or why argue or discuss?

Because that is how you learn and get to know newer things, a variety of things which you wouldn't know, wouldn't have thought of in the first place, or find a newer perspective on something you saw only through one lens, while it could have been seen through many. The debate culture which I intend to imbibe in each and everyone is very simple and very rewarding too.

Everybody needs to find that one individual (could be more than one too) among their known ones with whom they can argue over anything and are sure that the particular individual won't step back and will fight till the end of the line. I will give my example.

That person for me is UK (initials of course). He has known and seen me from when I was a child. He literally gives points to non-beatable points. I am not saying all of our arguments are right or make sense, but we don't stop until one accepts the other person's viewpoint. The topics are random and sometimes the most basic of all. It has helped both of us gain new perspectives over many things.

Importantly, generally, people think the way I talk is a bit harsh and my tone seems angrier, but the fact is that it's just my voice now. I also tend to use a lot of hand gestures and the more the points I have, more the louder I get and use a lot of gestures. If I don't do that, I don't feel like I am talking or that it isn't me basically.

Anybody looking from the outside would surely think why is this person shouting, but UK knows how I talk and argue and also understands it. During that period, anything goes and it is to be taken at face value and not at heart. Our arguments look like two idiots brawling verbally. Any point, however farfetched or imaginary or hypothetical, is valid. Anything and everything can be used as long as some sense is made out of it.

What others may find idiotic and difficult to comprehend, we try to understand what the other person wants to say and so we do not focus on how it is said or what words are used.

It's always been debate, never competition, no winning or losing. The method's very simple: select a topic, argue and don't stop until one understands the other or when both agree on the same point, i.e. neutral. Then move on to the next topic, but never is a topic unresolved.

I have argued the same way with my school friends and when I give random points to them like how I do with UK, they call me KK and then we all laugh. (It is extremely fun banter between my friends).

It was during one argument with UK, did I gain a new perspective which I turned into another theory and I have named it as **"The New Dish Effect"**. Let me explain,

Supposedly there is a dish that you haven't tried, so do you know how it tastes? Do you know what that dish feels like or what kind of senses it activates or brings in?

No, only after trying out the food do you get to know what it tastes like, how it should be eaten, what part of the brain it activates etc. Until then, you can only assume, by the smell or by the looks, what that dish could taste like, but it isn't necessary that what you assume is true.

Same way, without knowing what the other person actually feels about something or what that person is going through, don't strait up judge. Don't point out immediately and harshly; what they are doing is wrong until it is absolutely necessary (and maybe if the situation requires you to be tough). What you assume "could be" right is not necessarily right.

Don't speak & judge when you aren't in their shoes. Yeah, you can have your own thoughts about it but it isn't necessary to articulate or verbalize them. And that is where debate with that person ("the one") would help.

It would help because there you could discuss things freely and, because you have, you now know whether it should be told or not or if the words will be taken out of context or twisted. That person won't twist, but if he/she doesn't understand, he/she will just ask you to explain that argument again.

Because you have spoken about it and have understood it from at least one other person's viewpoint, you see everything and analyze it through multiple lenses. Debate helps improve our communication, understanding, listening and many other skills and helps maintain neutrality.

I'll give you another example which is deeply rooted in history and culture and will make you think about it for sure. Let me explain how.

The Mahabharata is one of the two biggest and widest believed Sanskrit epic poems of ancient India.

The Bhagavad Gita, is an episode recorded in the Mahabharata and is composed in the form of a dialogue between Prince Arjuna and Krishna, an avatar (incarnation) of the god Vishnu.

Do you know the same thing which we are discussing right now is done in this epic too?

Yeah, so basically, the Gita is just a conversation between Lord Krishna and Arjuna. Arjuna asks questions & puts forth his doubts and views/points while Krishna is answering and clearing them out for him.

What do you think that is? It's a discussion (debate). That is how Arjuna gets to know that the war was essential and cannot be escaped. Lord Krishna also has discussions with Karna, Dronacharya and Bheeshma.

So even gods had discussions and cleared things out, learned new things that way. It's been happening in our history all along.

Only when you discuss do you get answers and a newer approach/perspective. I am not saying all of this is true or false, but what I do know is, there are texts, those texts that are widely trusted among many throughout the world, which prove that when you discuss things you learn.

While the use of the "New Dish Effect" works in various contexts, conversely, at times it's vital that you don't eat the dish, not try it and also suggest the same to others. Some dishes should not be tried and it's better to assume and judge that it won't be good. Sometimes you need to do harsh things. It doesn't necessarily mean that you are a bad person or your thoughts are such. "Sometimes the good guys have to do bad things to make the bad guys pay". This quote makes a lot of sense. It's from Suits, a television series created and written by Aaron Korsh.

You get to know about people, their ideologies and perspectives only by talking to them and listening to them.

Practice makes perfect. It goes for anything from sports to studies to what not. The same way, you improve your talking/speaking skills by; you guessed it right, talking. To be able to talk to anyone is a skill and that skill you improve or cultivate by talking to your known ones, arguing about anything and everything with them, learning what they say, taking down their tips on where to go lower in tone, where to go higher, so that's why I recommend each and everyone to find that person/group with whom you can debate.

What debate also teaches you and this is very important to understand rebelliousness, to know when to not talk or argue, when to stay silent and let the other parties get it, win (The converse aspect of the new dish effect) because just being rebelliousness isn't enough, it is going to get you into trouble a lot of times or being that way could hurt someone, even someone close. Sometimes, as mentioned earlier, that you need to rebel against yourself to not rebel.

These few aforementioned lines can be summarized in different perspectives in a few quotes, such as, one mentioned by Abraham Lincoln.

"Better to remain silent and be thought a fool than to speak and remove all doubt"

And

"It's a dangerous thing, to mistake speaking without thought, for speaking the truth."

The first quote is as simple as it can get. At times, its better, to you know, stay silent and not open your mouth. There will be situations where you will realize that the opposite party actually doesn't possess the maturity or the emotional stability needed for the argument and it is better you stay quiet and let him take charge and win rather than making a fool of yourself.

The second one is from a movie titled Glass Onion: A Knives Out Mystery, which highlights that sometimes truth is harsh and its always better to give it a thought before actually uttering it.

But it isn't necessary to lie. If you can escape the situation on a technicality or wordplay, it's better to use it and leave. Sometimes technicality and lawyerism work. It helps bring a neutral stop point, which at times is heavily required.

All this you learn from speaking and debating and understanding what needs to be said, when and where. There's a time and place for everything. So find that individual or group with whom you can speak the way I speak with UK or Arjuna speaks with Lord Krishna.

So debates, discuss, argue, talk through, dispute, and go back and forth. Basically talk AWAY!!

Don't agree & accept immediately

This title "don't agree & accept immediately", I follow it heavily. Like there're very slim chances that I agree immediately, but I am always ready to listen and am always open and understand the fact that I could be wrong, but I still need to have some kind of argument or some discussion over the slightest of topics, because that is how I operate and most importantly, it's fun for me. Not fights or actual big debates but just some discussion as to whether it is actually the way it should be [the sentence] One of my friends would say in Tamil "Ivan thiruntha maatan, KK maari pesadha" (English translation being, "You will not change, you are a KK"). We have a good laugh about it.

That attitude is very important and that is the closest meaning of the rebellious spirit that you don't accept without some work or proof or conclusion.

Sometimes all you require is to stand your ground and say "No, you are wrong", to the opposite party (could be you yourself) and then prove to them why you are not ready to accept.

Steven Spielberg, one of the most if not the most commercially successful director, of films like Indiana Jones, was rejected out of film school 3 times. That does not mean he let it get to his head. If he did, he wouldn't have been where he is right now. You need to build your attitude that way to make sure that you don't agree with what the world says in general about you.

I will give you a real life example of what we are speaking about and this is one of my friends from high school. So we are commerce students and there are subjects like accountancy and economics. He didn't do well. He used to fail, but not once was he sad, because once he told me that this was not his field and it was design, i.e. UI/UX. So he took commerce because, for him, it was a no-brainer that he wasn't taking science. He just wanted to finish school. Now he has completed his course in UI/UX and is one of the first in my group to get a job and is happy.

Our professor used to say study or else it would be difficult for you. Studying that (commerce) was difficult for him, he didn't agree with the part where he isn't good or that the door is closed for him, because he knew where his passion lied and that's what he cared for.

That is what rebelliousness is. To find passion or things that you want to do, instead of asking the world and searching for it and then being sad that it did not pan out. Why not start doing things just like that? Randomly do something/some course/ try some food/ or if have an idea for a venture or start-up-execute it. If it fails or if you don't like it, don't simply accept that is the end for you. It's just that the particular thing you tried wasn't your cup of tea or you weren't interested in it or it did not pan out in that try.

The simpler phrase of the above lines is "Never give up". Both basically mean the same, except, this one sounds motivational and the other sounds rationally harsh. That's why I have added the word "immediately" in the title of this chapter; because it clarifies that it's plainly not disagreement but introspection first, then understanding whether the particular notion is agreeable or not.

During one of our arguments (between UK & me), he said something and then I shared my perspective which changed his way of thinking completely and now he uses my perspective and says it is better than what it was before.

So he said something about a situation not being right at the moment and not being able to rectify mistakes, being backlogged and having no help or something like that. He explained it like this.

"Think you are inside a deep pit hole and there is nothing else to do and you aren't able to escape and now the only way is if god helps (in the form of rain where he can swim up or something else like that). In real life, rain symbolizes somebody's help.

So when I heard this, the first thought was, and I said to him, if you are stuck in a hole with nothing to do, why not try to escape. Even if you fail, it's not like it is going to get worse. You will still stay inside. So, either things will be the same or they can only change for the better, not the worse.

Why wait for god, why wait for somebody's hand? You can always keep trying. I am not saying that you will succeed or life will improve, but you won't be stagnant. You will always have to do something. If you are in a pit hole, try scraping the walls and who knows that could work or try climbing or shouting or something. Basically not stopping but trying instead of just holding hands and sitting doing nothing.

When he heard this he was like, yeaaaah, and it changed his ideology completely. You got to put in the work and not think about the result or what's the point when it isn't going to bear fruit. The quote below perfectly describes the sentences above.

"Nothing in life is easy and if it's easy it isn't meaningful and if it is meaningful it isn't easy."

Also, speaking of quotes and proverbs, not all are always right. Some proverbs need to get updated with time because at the time they were phrased and the times we are in right now, things have changed and changed drastically. The easiest example I can think of is "Money can't buy happiness". Don't simply agree with it without actually thinking.

This quote is wrong in itself. No, money can buy happiness, but the thing here is, it depends. Materialistic happiness, definitely yes it can buy. While you zoom in on the quote there will be exceptions. Ask somebody who is in debt about what money is for him, provide him with money. It gets him both materialistic and immaterialistic happiness.

Shah Rukh Khan, an actor, also speaks about this and is a good example for many of the sentences used in this book. He also believes that "money can't buy happiness" is a flawed statement. He doesn't just simply agree to anything without actually giving it a serious thought. He wanted to be a sportsperson, but injuries didn't allow him, so he did something else. He didn't stop. He considers himself as his competition and not anybody else and that the only fight he has is with him. He can't compete with everybody, there will always be somebody who looks better, acts better or does everything better, but what he can do is rebel against his previous version to be the better version every day. He has the never give up attitude, doesn't hesitate from trying something new and has shown that numerous times with his films and other ventures. And it isn't like he has not failed. No, he has failed many times, but now he also has that experience where he has failed and, because he has failed now, he now knows what not to do. So keep trying and doing, work on it and accept that you don't have to accept everything.

Unclog your mind, tap in the potential and start taking challenges.

Ready to accept and agree

Everything we have discussed until now has been about reaching success or how to reach or achieve it.

But what happens if you fail?

This is the part nobody talks about because that doesn't provide motivation but rather creates doubts and that is the harsh reality, the inevitable truth that there are higher chances that you could fail. So, in this section, we discuss rebelliousness and those failures.

Before we jump into detail, there is a perfect movie line which talks about this topic and that movie is Chhichhore, a Hindi language movie directed by Nitesh Tiwari. A movie based on life, losing, studies, friendships and many other things.

The protagonist of the movie says this line

"Success ke baad ka plan sabke pass hai

(Everyone has a plan for, after success)

lekin agar galti se fail ho gaaye

(But if you fail even by mistake)

toh failure se kaise deal karna hai

(Then how to deal with that failure)

koi baat hi nahi karna chahtha"

(No one wants speaks about it.)

So is it guaranteed that you will succeed? No, so what happens if you fail? Many think that is the end of it and then there is nothing left.

You are completely wrong and a fool if you think that. Think of the first example we used in this book, about a baby learning to walk.

Okay, so you started learning to walk and you fell down a few times, so are you not walking now? Did you say you are done; this isn't my cup of tea? No, you failed that time, that specific time, but you tried again. Maybe failed again and again too, but ultimately, at one point you did walk. You knew falling was not the end. It all starts with the mindset.

It is what it is.

You failed, so what? Okay done, do something else; the year wasn't great, and so what? The coming ones would be. That assignment or sum didn't work out, try the formula again. You failed an exam, so write again. It's not the end of the world and yes, you will be hurt and you will feel sad or disappointed and down, but that does not mean it is over. Have a plan not only for success but failure too. Because not always will you succeed, but there will be a lot of times when you will fail. Don't give up then.

Why do you backup your phone data? The reason is you are scared that you may lose it. The same way, have a backup for scenarios where you fail. That way, you are prepared for the worst circumstances too. The ones who are calm during the storm are the ones who are fearless and have backup, for if they fail.

This is one thing that we can and should take a lot from the professionals & stars of the entertainment field. Because not all their movies are blockbusters. Some don't collect money, and are considered flops, but that doesn't stop them, they just think about it, brush it off and try to rectify the previous mistakes in the next or the next next.

You can't change it. It is what it is. The phrase doesn't simply mean accepting the stuff that has happened and working on it. It also means that you did your part, the uncontrollable factor came into play and you are just seeing it and reacting. You need to start accepting that. That's it. As contradictory as it is to the previous chapter, success does not have a formula that is based on logic or understandability. It is just success, which is its own explanation.

Once you start accepting the fact that there could be something wrong with the plan or with you, it is when you take the next & necessary step towards alienating that failure.

I have another theory for this (mind that, all the theories that I have created work out from my perspective. Just try seeing that way and i hope it helps), which I call **"The Addiction-Rehab Theory"**.

So consider that an individual smokes, and a lot too (Addiction). Others surrounding the individual are worried about the person and ask him/her to stop, but the individual does not see any wrong in his/her actions. Here the problem is that he/she isn't ready to see a different angle on their action but stuck to one single preview of perspective. So what I do is, I tell the person that "See, there are rehabs for drinking, smoking and many other things. There aren't any rehabs for drinking too much juice or, say, doing a lot of yoga. No, there are rehabs only for stuff like drugs or drinking or smoking etc. So, if there are rehabs only for stuff like that, it means that there is a purpose for having it and not there for juice. There must be something wrong about that addiction and not other ones."

What this does is, creates a sense of thinking for the individual and, therefore, they start to realize that, yeah, something could be wrong about it. This theory only helps one accept that there could be something wrong and acceptance is the first and foremost step in rehabilitation or victory or change.

One needs to be ready to accept that they could fail and probably will many times, but that is not the end of it. It is just that the way they chose that specific try did not work out. A clear cut perfect example would be Colonel Sanders.

Everyone knows about KFC, their famous chicken and the recipe and the delicious taste. He got it right at the age of 62, with the chicken recipe not selling for like 1000 times before it hit off. And not only that, he did not do well in other careers before KFC also, like lawyer and salesperson jobs also did not pan out.

He tried and was ready to accept that something was not right and not going according to his plan, but maybe it was not his fault too. It is what it is. It is just that you have to give it your all. Nothing more, nothing less.

Conversely, sometimes you have to agree that the road chosen is not for you and you need to step out if it before it creates havoc. If you have seen the series, "The Big Bang Theory", created by Chuck Lorre and Bill Prady, you would get this and for those who don't, I would try to explain this as clearly as possible.

Penny (character) wants to become an actress and works for it too, but at one point she knows that it isn't happening or this isn't for her, so she jumps ship to a different career and makes it work and becomes rather good at it whereas Sheldon (character) is a physicist who, even after ups and downs sticks to string theory (even he tries to jump ship but his heart does not follow) and finally finds success and wins the Nobel.

As a baby, you had everything or you did everything the book says, you had that rebellious thought, you put up a fight, you got the satisfaction and it would be visible on your face and your perspective is just there, on point. As a baby you didn't care about failure, even if you did, you would do the same thing again. It happened only because, as a baby our senses aren't fine tuned to think or over think but, just on "Do", doing the work

To succeed you also need to fail, it is just a game of snake and ladder and your job is only to roll the dice (work on your need/goal/want) and stick with the game. You win, you lose, and you try again. All you need is contradiction, working for your side, i.e. for you and when needed, helping you contradict everything else on the path. That is what is ready to accept things, agree is.

Finally, the way you build rebelliousness is to do.

Do

It is very much self-explanatory and really very simple. This is the one thing that everyone in the world who has achieved success would say or actually anybody would. All the rest all is the backend work and this is the front end work, which is visible and the main element.

There's a movie called Top Gun: Maverick, directed by Joseph Kosinski, which clearly showcases the fact of don't think, just do. Sometimes, when we start to think and analyze before doing something, we tend to over think and procrastinate and that is what delays or denies success. At those times, all you need is a simple phrase in your mind, "Just Do". You may have the best idea in the world, but it is of no value if you do not act upon it. There could be many reasons that you don't. Sometimes you may think that because you haven't touched that yet, that project is something that you have not wasted or screwed (this I saw from a series called "How I Met Your Mother") and it does make sense at the moment, but when you think about it, you are just scared of rejection and failure and that won't lead you anywhere forward except to disappointment & regret.

Most of the time or situations I have seen people not do things; it is due to a single reason. They say they don't know how. They say they do not know that particular thing or they do not have the right skill or so.

For scenarios like these, I have created another theory which helps me stop procrastination, over thinking or sometimes under thinking and just take the leap of faith and jump.

The theory is called **"The ABC Law"**. It is basically a theory which reinforces the "do" factor in me.

So, when you first started school or studying more precisely, you did not know the alphabet. So are you speaking or writing now? Yes, you are speaking and you know how to write. You didn't know it then, but you did learn it. The thought did not stop you and now it is like that is how you speak, like a body part which was ever present.

Same way, there are things that you don't know or won't know, just like alphabet, but so what? Just learn it. Do, take part in the process, and then use that skill to do the next bit and then the next and then the next.

Up skill yourself to the point where idea meets execution to create reality.

You may have heard the old twig/sticks story, where the grandfather asks his grandson to break that bundle, but however he tried he couldn't, then when asked how to do it , the old man said to break them few at a time.

The same way, your final idea point can't be achieved in just one go. Try breaking the ingredients/work into plausible ones and break each one, then go the next. It is always about the process and not the result.

If you focus on the uncontrollables, then you aren't moving, they control you, but when you put all your focus on the controllable aspects, then you are in the driver's seat and you are in control of them.

Say, for example, you have an idea for a mobile application and you think that it is a game changer. Why haven't you started your work on it? So you don't know how to build an application. Learn how to, take some course, hire somebody, ask a friend. Don't sit idle. Don't give yourselves false hopes by saying it will happen; it won't unless you do it. What you seek isn't seeking you. The end goal stays the same, it is always constant. It isn't moving towards you, but you are or should move towards it.

There are literally a million examples to prove that, you have to step up and just do it. Not worry about mistakes, because that is the harsh reality that not all you do is going to be a successful venture. You will fail. Do it again.

Anyone in the fitness field is the primary example of this. You won't get the body you desire until you start doing, start somewhere, like go the gym consistently, maintain a proper food diet, sleep cycle and do the things that get you to where you want to go/be. Want a six-pack clear cut biscuit abs? Take control of your body fat. Exercise based on it. You can't just buy abs like you get chips from a supermarket.

If you aren't achieving something, most likely the chances are that you haven't done it right or haven't done it in the first place. There are and will be times when you put or give in your everything-1000%, but won't get what you want, but at that time, the one thing that you should keep in mind is that the uncontrollables came into work, not your work ethic. So chin up and go at it. You weren't at the right place at the right time that particular time doesn't mean that you never will.

If you only focus on uncertainty, then that would drive you crazy. You have done your part, find another part to create or fix or amend and let uncertainty run its course.

So that's what I have done too, and I am no way near perfect, like I am on the first step to reaching something (doing) that would help me reach/achieve perfectness and success.

 Also, you define your metrics and perfectness, so don't compare yours with others or somebody else's with another one. You are there to rule, not compete, and if there's a competition it's with yourself. Try to be better than yesterday and that requires doing things.

My challenge was to write a book and finish it and while doing so, I was like, why should you have certain criteria or academic knowledge for you to put up words and perspective. The goal was to write a book, publish it and promote it, and for a person, who isn't into books, I have rebelled against myself and I'll publish this and show it to my family and friends and known ones. And beyond that, if it reaches an audience and helps somebody become better or helps anyone in any way, that would be one of the biggest achievements of my life, not that it wasn't before (as in being able to write and publish it itself is a success for me).

So take that first step or jump towards your goal by doing stuff. Try that dish you always wanted to, play that game, write that book, create the short film you wanted, give the audition you're thinking about, give up some kind of addiction you have or take the first step in getting rid of it, anything except staying stagnant. Even starting to think differently is doing things.

Once you start doing, you are the god/the helping hand you are wishing you wanted/needed or are wanting/needing, while being in that pit hole.(Harry saving Sirius & himself, Harry Potter and the Prisoner of Azkaban, a movie based on the book by J.K. Rowling of the same name.)

Just Do it. (Nike, Yeah I know too)

Thoughts to ponder

These are just random thoughts and stuff which I think and sometimes think, why are people thinking this or not thinking this?

- Are having goals or some higher ambition from life the way people are to be judged. Because sometimes some people are like just blank, never wanting anything or not wanting. They just want to live to the end normally no expectation

  Isn't it okay just to wander through life finding interesting things just see through also a goal?

- Living a normal life should give you chills. If you haven't done something out of yours then the potential is just gone to waste isn't it? I always say this to myself that if you are just as regular as the next person then what the point is. If you are unique, you should look & be too.

- You know about the rabbit/duck illusion we talked about earlier so you know that it isn't necessary what you see, others should see too. Doesn't same thing apply for almost anything in the world, then why is it not the case?

- If change is the only constant, then basically everything/everyone is evolving. Then in a way is trust coming under it. My father always says "Never trust anybody especially yourself". I know he means it in a general term like stand on your own like types but that led to me thinking.

- I have seen a lot of reels and posts saying that surround you with positive people and positivity. What I feel is you need to surround yourself with real people, who can tell practical real things. Not all things work out and when you only think positive then you tend to think that it will work out.

  No, the way should be, "Don't think negative, but anticipate and always have an option that things could go wrong. Don't expect but anticipate disappointment so that when that actually happens you are ready but when it doesn't you are elated".

- Why are some 1000 year old proverbs still used? I mean like in that particular era it worked but in the present scenario does it actually stay true? There can be the fact that it still holds meaning but the words don't or it is just you, trying to make something out of nothing.

An easy example would be is the statement that I read today "You can't cheat an honest man". Easily arguable and guilty, don't you think?

- If presently there are resources available at will and the internet has become like the greatest open book. How did the ones before internet actually work through and get somewhere. Their work holds more depth is it or not?

- If you play a game and a siren goes off in the game, it means that you are doing something wrong and the sound is the warning. Not being content with the present knowing that if you put in the effort you are capable of, you can be much more. So isn't discontentment and not being happy right now the way you are, the motivation/warning of the game of life.

- What you seek isn't seeking you and sometimes it is vice versa. Simple example is you trying to find something in your house say a nail cutter. Think

- How can you become the person that you wish to be unless you live the life that you wish not to live? Or to say if you want to see a rainbow you got to put up with rain first.

- Why are you trying to fit in when you actually were born to stand out? The theme of this book based on a movie dialogue and when you think about it makes sense.

- If you could change something about you, then you wouldn't be you, don't you think? It is more important to automatically evolve then force.

-

PS: a blank bullet because that is for you. Everyone has some thoughts or ideas or theories they think/ponder about; I have mine some of which I have written here. That blank space means that you can have as many and should and also should think about it too.

Conclusion

Why do you guys think I have written this conclusion over here? This is a book rather than, say a college project, but the reason here is, to let you know that the only conclusion here is

That whatever change you need is based on your work and whatever you have understood from this book is based on your interpretation and not my writing. Hope that this makes you reach places you never thought existed, but those places do exist and the only barrier is your mind.

If change is the only constant, let that constant be at the top of mountains, not at the bottom of the sea.

Your limit is the universe, because even the sky has a limit, but the universe is unlimited because, as of now, we do not know how much else is out there.

So bring change in your universe and help others bring change in theirs.

Motivational Stuff

I consider this as a cliché because everyone now provides it, but these lines do invoke a sense of thought and action. This section is just quotes, movie dialogues, reels that I remember and like that provide self-belief and brings on that "doing things" spirit.

IMPORTANT NOTICE:

Do you know what the key ingredient is that lacks in all the motivational stuff?

The fact is that while they help bring a mindset or belief, they don't help a lot in making you do or get started with something because they are not connected with a real life example which has happened in your life or around you, i.e. friends, family, teachers or colleagues or even strangers for that fact. Using examples is extremely important because that helps us ground big things into our normal reality and we get a sense of connect with that reality. So connect the statement with real life and see the change.

SO LET'S GO,

- → It is what it is.
- → The worst hell I can think of is that when you die, the person you became meets the person you could have become.----- Frank Mir
- → Life isn't fair and it isn't just candy land or wonderland. Deal with it, don't cry over it or make a fuss. It is in spite of that what you do that leads you to satisfaction & happiness
- → Social media is such a place where if you say "Water is very important for

life", someone will get offended and reply "Tell this to people who lost their dear ones in flooding".

→ Feeling sad after making a decision doesn't mean it is a bad decision.

→ The cards are dealt so no fuss over crying on it. Work around the dealt ones and play & react to the room.

→ The more you learn, the less you know, widely known as the wisdom paradox.

→ Boredom sparks creativity

→ Never put passion before principles. Even if you win you lose. ----- Mr. Miyagi, the Karate Kid Part II.

→ Rest at the end not in the middle. ----- Kobe Bryant.

→ You always have a choice. ----- Michelle Hodkin.

→ Be tough but fair.

→ Win a no win situation by rewriting the rules – Kobayashi Maru, training exercise in the Star Trek franchise.

→ You only die once, you live everyday and each day you become your own doppelganger. ----- 9/11 Responder Advocate John Feal & Ted Mosby, How I met your mother.

→ Don't ever let someone tell you, you can't do something. Not even me. You got a dream, you got to protect it. People can't do something themselves, they want to tell you can't do it. You want something, go get it. Period. ----- Chris Gardener.

→ Perfectness is a myth. No one is ever perfect nor can one become.

→ A thread once cut in two or how many ever can never be joined back without

a knot. It will always have a bump.
Work & deal with it.

→

And the line which I have invented for myself
and use as a look through lens is

INITIATE – INNOVATE – IMPROVISE

For me it works wonders and comprises
everything said in this book. Just give it your
own meaning.

PS: a blank bullet because, that is for your
motivational/inspirational quotes. Everyone
has their own favorite ones; I have mine some
of which I have written here.

Acknowledgments

Just before ending the book, I would add the fact that while this is completely my perspective, there are reasons for me having that and am thankful for the reasons/people due to which/whom I gained it.

First, as always, I am thankful to my family. Because they brought me up and now if I have typed this out it is because of the resources and knowledge they provided me with. Second, I thank the staff of my father's shop, they are like an extended family and among them one is UK (mentioned earlier), and the rest are MA, PSA & BA. I have used initials for no reason. I just like it this way.

I am grateful for the situations I grew up in and the way I was brought up. If not for those situations and scenarios, I wouldn't be me. I do not know the words that would help me say what I want to say.

I am thankful to each and every one of my friends because, half of the time I have spent in my life is either in school or college, with these guys, so the way I talk & think has evolved and I have learnt from them a lot too, but don't worry you will always be idiots. (Have to insult after a compliment, unsaid rule)

PS: The ones who get this, you are too a **KK**, doesn't change a damn thing.

I am thankful to the internet, television and social media apps (mainly Instagram) because that is how I watched movies and shows, got to know about celebs and successful people, the accounts that have posts, the reels, the videos that I saw that enhanced me, inspired me and helped me gain a new perspective and understanding of myself.

Also, I would like to thank my teachers because almost all the time I have wanted to argue what they said, so that helped me get new points and POVs about a particular thing which led to some other topic and perspective too[sometimes me being right but a lot of time getting to know that they are right too.]

If I have forgotten anyone else, thank you too.

Also, if it does ever, become like a selling book in advance, a big big BIG thanks to you for buying and reading it. I hope this book brings the best of things for you ahead.

Also, unknowingly, if I have forgotten to attribute or thank anybody, mainly to all those Instagram accounts that I don't remember, I would like to thank them.

About the Author

Nothing much to say about me, a 21-year-old with crazy weird theories and arguments and who just likes to do things that are challenging. Plus, by reading this, you will get to know about me a little, what my thought process is and stuff. My name's Sidhanth. I am from Chennai, Tamil Nadu, India (that is why the reference to South Indian food).

I don't think I have anything else to write in this section, because there is actually nothing much to say. So, if you do have like anything to ask, then I am more comfortable because that is something I can answer. Just, out of nothing or nowhere, it is very difficult for me to describe myself or write about.

"I know of no better life purpose than to perish in attempting the great and the impossible.

The fact that something seems impossible shouldn't be a reason to not pursue it. That's exactly what makes it worth pursuing it.

Where would the courage and greatness be if success was certain and there was no risk?

The only true failure is shrinking away from life's challenges "

<u>Friedrich Nietzsche</u>